Little RIDDLERS

Derbyshire

Edited By Sarah Washer

First published in Great Britain in 2018 by:

Young**Writers**

Young Writers
Remus House
Coltsfoot Drive
Peterborough
PE2 9BF
Telephone: 01733 890066
Website: www.youngwriters.co.uk

FOREWORD

Dear Reader,

Are you ready to get your thinking caps on to puzzle your way through this wonderful collection?

Young Writers' Little Riddlers competition set out to encourage young writers to create their own riddles. Their answers could be whatever or whoever their imaginations desired; from people to places, animals to objects, food to seasons. Riddles are a great way to further the children's use of poetic expression, including onomatopoeia and similes, as well as encourage them to 'think outside the box' by providing clues without giving the answer away immediately.

All of us here at Young Writers believe in the importance of inspiring young children to produce creative writing, including poetry, and we feel that seeing their own riddles in print will keep that creative spirit burning brightly and proudly.

We hope you enjoy riddling your way through this book as much as we enjoyed reading all the entries.

CONTENTS

Leighton Michael James Boyce (7)   59
Joshua Stanley (7)   60
Sophie Louise Willett (7)   61
Benjamin Taylor (7)   62
Ryan Myers-King (6)   63
Summer Jacqueline Maureen Heald (6)   64
Lewis Lomas (6)   65
Archie Quinlan (6)   66
Reuben Atkinson (7)   67
Freddie Hughes-Couper (6)   68
Haniya Hussain (6)   69

Normanton House School, Derby

Nusaybah Naseer (6)   70
Abdullah Mahfuz (6)   71
Azka Bhatti (7)   72
Zahra Yasir (6)   73
Sumayyah Hussain (6)   74

Renishaw Primary School, Sheffield

Addison Homyard (7)   75
Scarlett Fay Green (6)   76
Ella Bradshaw (7)   77
Kelsi-Rae Deakin (6)   78
Edie Bonewell (7)   79
Pixie Pears (7)   80
Hollie Mae Williams (7)   81
Kai Paul Taylor (7)   82
Elissa Summer Bentley (6)   83
Jessica Elizabeth Cusack (7)   84
Elliot Forrest (6)   85
Isabella Hurst (6)   86
Willow-Rose Bullock (7)   87
Miley Marie Grainger (6)   88
Daniel Robson (6)   89
Felicity Lewis-Ord (7)   90
Rio Poulton (7)   91
Harvey Watson (6)   92
Callum Halliday (6)   93

Damien Paul Wilkinson-Yates (7)   94
Tiffany Lindley (7)   95

Stenson Fields Primary Community School, Stenson Fields

Italia Shuttleworth Fulton (7)   96
Naiya Raichura (7)   97
Ana Karamihaleva (6)   98
David Jagosz (6)   99
Bobby Griffiths (6)   100
Saraya Thind (7)   101
Myraa Khan (6)   102
Amelia Ridley (6)   103
Tilly Rose Dean (6)   104
Ava Gould (6)   105
Dylan Perkin (6)   106
Sophia Meek (6)   107
Avinash Singh Takhar (7)   108
Hollie Jennifer Pearce (5)   109
Freya Mae Chorley (6)   110
Kyla Turner (7)   111
Shreya Dhugga (6)   112
Ethan Child (7)   113
Ethan Dhariwal (6)   114
Ajay Janagal (6)   115
Parneet Shanan (7)   116
Evan Hall (6)   117
Ella Holland (5)   118
Skye Bareham (5)   119
Amelia Fulcher (6)   120
Rajan Singh Khatkar (6)   121
Nikolai Sheppard (6)   122
Freya Turner (5)   123
Paige Buxton (6)   124
Kenzie Maneffa (7)   125
Mitchel Samuel Victor Brownson (7)   126
Esmé Evelyn Fernley (7)   127
Liam Whyatt (6)   128
Amelia (6)   129
Zach Coleman-Wright (6)   130
Arniya Chopra (6)   131

Arun Singh Mehat (6)	132	Edith Beatrice Ford (6)	172
Olivia Rose Borrington (6)	133	Maisie Ann White (7)	173
Khloe Ann Walker (5)	134	Marnie Learmouth (7)	174
Corben Jozef Wensierski (7)	135		
Musaab Abdulghani Elazreg (6)	136		
Amber Brewin (6)	137		
Olivier Siemieński (5)	138		
Ethan Michael Haywood (6)	139		
Ethan Brealey (5)	140		
Tyler Baldwin (5)	141		
Harvey Bloor (6)	142		
Lilly May Hamilton (7)	143		
Layla Callanan (6)	144		
Maison Levi Squires (6)	145		
Harleen Kaur-Samra (5)	146		
Alfie James Page (6)	147		
Shanice Mfarinya (5)	148		
Reuben Kyle Pall (6)	149		
Blake Horton (7)	150		
Ruby Horton (7)	151		
Brody Rocco Lawlor (6)	152		
Shanae Mfarinya (5)	153		
Darai Stewart-Chance (5)	154		
Andreas Ferreira (6)	155		
Sam Murby (6)	156		
Raheem Mahmood (6)	157		
Evie Read (5)	158		
Katelin Eason-Patilla (5)	159		
Aleah Shanker (5)	160		
Ciaran Gilligan (7)	161		

Wirksworth Federation Of Infant Schools, North End

Finn Poyser (7)	162
Reece John Gregory (7)	163
Finley Flitter (6)	164
Isaac Vega-White (6)	165
Billy Rooney (7)	166
Edward Lowery (7)	167
Ava Sophia Bennett (6)	168
William Eaton (7)	169
Anya Neve McCabe (7)	170
Kieran Gregory (6)	171

THE POEMS

Fantastic Flyer

I fly in the big, blue sky.
I have very long wings.
I have a big pointy tail and a strong body.
I have a flat bottomed body.
I normally make loud noises.
I have a little engine at the back of me.
What am I?

Answer: An aeroplane.

Nathan Stuart (7)
Bakewell CE Infant School, Bakewell

Scary Stuff

I never miss my prey.
I eat giraffes because they are my prey.
I am king of the jungle.
I have more fur on my face than a tiger.
I don't have stripes.
I look like a tiger without stripes.
What am I?

Answer: A lion.

Theo Sexton (6)
Bakewell CE Infant School, Bakewell

Speedy Wheels!

I have brakes and wheels.
You can make me go.
You can ride on me.
You have to push me to make me go fast.
You can get me in different colours.
You can get me from the shop.
What am I?

Answer: A scooter.

Ella Jess Wood (6)
Bakewell CE Infant School, Bakewell

Chompy Chomp

I live in water.
You can't find me up high in the sky.
I eat my prey.
I don't smile at people.
I'm green and dangerous.
My teeth go snap and chomp.
What am I?

Answer: A crocodile.

Imogen Casey (7)
Bakewell CE Infant School, Bakewell

Underground Tunnels!

I might pop up and say hello.
You might see me sometimes.
I might be in your garden.
I wiggle down and make holes.
I wiggle down and down.
I never stop wiggling.
What am I?

Answer: A worm.

Charlotte Hamilton (7)
Bakewell CE Infant School, Bakewell

Slithery Secrets

I make an exciting pet.
You sometimes see me in the trees.
I might hug you tight!
I'm not furry.
I'm watching you sneakily.
My body is super long.
What am I?

Answer: A python.

Luka Price (6)
Bakewell CE Infant School, Bakewell

Magic

I have a skirt and a top.
I live at the bottom of your garden.
I have a wand.
And I have sparkly high heels.
I have magic dust.
I have pretty wings.
What am I?

Answer: A fairy.

Isabella Kirkwood (7)
Bakewell CE Infant School, Bakewell

Chomp Secret

I stomp through the forest.
I hide behind trees.
I eat other animals.
I am not a crocodile.
I don't make a lot of noise.
I live in a swamp.
What am I?

Answer: An alligator.

William MacLaurin (6)
Bakewell CE Infant School, Bakewell

Cute!

I am cute and fluffy.
I have a fluffy tail.
I have a cute body.
I have four cute paws.
I have seven whiskers.
Sometimes I get furious and I growl.
What am I?

Answer: A cat.

Holly Hope Marriott (6)
Bakewell CE Infant School, Bakewell

Amazing To Eat

I have a tasty flavour.
I can be cut up.
I can be shaped like an egg.
I make your teeth rotten.
I am brown, black or white.
I can be buttons.
What am I?

Answer: Chocolate.

Charlie Mellor (6)
Bakewell CE Infant School, Bakewell

Slimy

I am slimy.
I jump really high.
My babies can swim.
I eat yummy flies.
I make a sound like a burp.
I leap forwards, backwards, left and right.
What am I?

Answer: A frog.

Freya Roose (7)
Bakewell CE Infant School, Bakewell

Vicious!

I am the most vicious animal in the world.
I have a long, furry tail.
I hunt for my own prey.
I don't have feelings.
I am orange and black.
What am I?

Answer: A tiger.

Fleur Lahiffe (6)
Bakewell CE Infant School, Bakewell

Fruit Power

I am yellowy-red.
I have a small stalk.
You may find me in a book by Roald Dahl.
I have a rock-hard stone.
I am so juicy.
I am a fruit.
What am I?

Answer: A peach.

Rosie Newbould (6)
Bakewell CE Infant School, Bakewell

Amazing Pet

I have legs that are fluffy.
I have two cute ears.
I hop really high.
I like to eat grass.
I like hopping.
I don't like people.
What am I?

Answer: A rabbit.

Jacob Hanby (6)
Bakewell CE Infant School, Bakewell

Pride Rock

I rule the jungle.
I have a mighty roar.
I am dangerous when I'm hungry.
I'm yellow and orange.
My stripes are big and fluffy.
What am I?

Answer: A tiger.

Harry Andrews (7)
Bakewell CE Infant School, Bakewell

Garden Pet

I have a tail.
I have floppy ears.
I have a fluffy body.
I have four white legs.
I have medium-sized feet.
I live in a hutch.
What am I?

Answer: A rabbit.

Eliza Janette Oliver (7)
Bakewell CE Infant School, Bakewell

In The Jungle

I am a type of cat.
I am a wild animal.
I sometimes live in a busy zoo.
I am a scary cat.
I am stripy.
I can roar very loud.
What am I?

Answer: A tiger.

Luna Hamlett (6)
Bakewell CE Infant School, Bakewell

Summer Time

I am similar to a heart.
I am rosy-red.
You eat me.
I have a short stalk.
I have black spots.
I lie on a bed of straw.
What am I?

Answer: A strawberry.

Ruby Eleanor Bown (6)
Bakewell CE Infant School, Bakewell

Chilly

I snow in my month.
You can play in me.
I am a cold season.
You can build snowmen in my season.
I come after autumn.
What am I?

Answer: Winter.

Lucy Harper (7)
Bakewell CE Infant School, Bakewell

Feathery Friend

I fly high in the sky.
I see you sleeping.
I am nocturnal.
I am out at night.
I am a bird.
I live in a tree.
What am I?

Answer: An owl.

Bella Wayne (7)
Bakewell CE Infant School, Bakewell

Delicious

I grow on the ground.
I have seeds.
I have a stalk.
I am red.
I taste yummy.
I come with jam.
What am I?

Answer: A strawberry.

Harry Taylor (7)
Bakewell CE Infant School, Bakewell

Leaves

I make you put on your coat.
I make leaves fall off the trees.
I am windy.
I am one of four.
What am I?

Answer: Autumn.

India Wilson-Crellin (6)
Bakewell CE Infant School, Bakewell

Zoom

I have wheels.
I have handlebars.
I have a chain.
I have brakes.
You can ride on me.
What am I?

Answer: A bike.

Charlie Simpson (6)
Bakewell CE Infant School, Bakewell

Pinky

I am very small.
I am a girl but not a human.
I am a royal princess.
I love flowers.
I am not an elf or pixie.
I am pink with tall, pink hair.
What am I?

Answer: *The troll princess.*

Naomi Lee (6)
Emmanuel School, Derby

Freezing People

I have a bright pink hat
And a big, smiley face.
I have lovely grey buttons
And I have sticks for my arms and legs.
I come alive in the winter.
What am I?

Answer: A snowman.

Hadassah Iyanuoluwa Adeyemo (7)
Emmanuel School, Derby

Ice-Cold

I am ice-cold.
I can be hard or smooth.
I have many different colours.
I like fruit and sweet things.
I taste yummy.
You can scoop me.
What am I?

Answer: An ice cream.

Abigail Fraser (6)
Emmanuel School, Derby

Night Creeper

I am the fastest runner.
I make life more fun.
I am a night creeper,
A jewel stealer.
I am a sword fighter.
My feet make me lighter.
Who am I?

Answer: A ninja.

Elanor Ruth Snowdon (6)
Emmanuel School, Derby

Mr Angry

I have four big legs,
Very sharp teeth and a spiky back.
I have a scary roar and angry eyes.
I have a short tail and am a fast runner.
What am I?

Answer: A dinosaur.

Malachi Reid (6)
Emmanuel School, Derby

Cold

I am round.
I wear clothes but I'm cold.
I like carrots.
I am white but I feel blue.
I can be big or small.
I melt away.
What am I?

Answer: A snowman.

Juliana Cox (5)
Emmanuel School, Derby

Big Cat

I have a hairy tail.
I am strong.
I have a yellow face.
I roar loudly.
I have a sort of hairy head.
My teeth are sharp.
What am I?

Answer: A lion.

Akili Urassa (6)
Emmanuel School, Derby

Fast

I have a silver suit
And fight with lots of people.
I am really strong
And I have a sharp sword.
Sometimes I ride a horse.
What am I?

Answer: A knight.

David Sarkodie (6)
Emmanuel School, Derby

Ice Cold

I am very white
And I have buttons on my chest.
I have wood for my arms.
Sometimes I wear a scarf
But in heat I can melt.
What am I?

Answer: A snowman.

Isaac Cyriac (6)
Emmanuel School, Derby

Black Warrior

High jumper.
I am a fierce fighter.
I am black all over.
I am a strong kicker.
I can smash wood.
Who am I?

Answer: A ninja.

Catherine-May Mugadza (7)
Emmanuel School, Derby

Pet Poem

I am a pet you can get.
I am so fluffy, you can cuddle me all night.
I am so fast you can't catch me.
I am so cute sometimes.
When you throw sticks, I catch them.
I woof when someone knocks on the door.
What am I?

Answer: A dog.

Thomas Miller (7)
FitzHerbert CE Primary School, Fenny Bentley

Colourful Riddle

I grow in a tree.
I grow in hot countries.
I am juicy.
My colour is also my name.
I can be a drink as well.
I can have pips inside.
What am I?

Answer: An orange.

Jack Lloyd Julian (7)
FitzHerbert CE Primary School, Fenny Bentley

What Am I?

I live in a very cold place.
I have flippers
And I live in the sea.
I have very sharp tusks.
I look like a whale.
What am I?

Answer: A walrus.

Grace Mae Stevenson (6)
FitzHerbert CE Primary School, Fenny Bentley

The Hard Riddle

I am made out of wood.
People read me.
I have pages.
I live on a shelf.
I have pictures.
I have words.
What am I?

Answer: A book.

George Henry Webb (5)
FitzHerbert CE Primary School, Fenny Bentley

Riddles From The Past

Slowly, I gobble my juicy, green plants and herbs because I'm a herbivore.
I live in the green jungle with lots of green herbs and dark green trees that I like to eat.
I'm dark grey and black.
I have sharp, pointy teeth like a sharp sword.
I have a long, thick and strong neck and black eyes.
I have big legs and a whippy tail.
I have sharp claws like a sword.
What am I?

Answer: A diplodocus.

Amber Jade Kaculi (7)
Hadfield Infant School, Hadfield

What Am I?

I am bigger than your hand.
I come from North America.
I eat high-growing plants.
I have teeth like cones.
I lived fifteen million years ago.
At first I was small, then I got bigger than the forest.
I sometimes stand on two legs.
I love stones to grind up my food.
At first I was an egg.
I weigh as much as two elephants.
What am I?

Answer: A diplodocus.

Evie Porter (7)
Hadfield Infant School, Hadfield

Years Gone By

Quickly, I eat juicy, green and small plants because I'm a hungry herbivore.
I have a long, tall neck as long as three giraffes' necks.
I have a small head as small as a football.
Slowly, I whip my big tail around to protect me.
You might find me in a herd as I'm weak.
If you are lucky, you might find me in a wonderful fossil.
What am I?

Answer: A diplodocus.

Phoebe Anne Lyons (6)
Hadfield Infant School, Hadfield

What Am I?

I pluck low-growing plants with my sharp teeth.
I charge at my enemy quickly and crossly.
I have the largest skull of any land animal.
I live in North America.
I have four thick, heavy legs.
I eat plants.
I have a tail like a horse.
I am smaller than a diplodocus.
What am I?

Answer: A triceratops.

Isabella Pearson (6)
Hadfield Infant School, Hadfield

What Am I?

I whip my armoured tail around to hit other
dinosaurs.
I do not fly or swim.
I eat plants, so I am a herbivore.
I have an armoured tail.
I am a little bit like a stegosaurus.
I hatched from an egg.
I have spikes on my armour.
I live in Canada and Asia.
What am I?

Answer: An ankylosaurus.

Sophia Carr (7)
Hadfield Infant School, Hadfield

Years Gone By

I live in the deep, dark forest and the hot, dry desert.
I live in the bottom of North America.
I can be eaten by bigger dinosaurs.
I am a ferocious carnivore and I can eat four humans whole.
I have four legs.
If you're lucky, you may find me in hard rock.
What am I?

Answer: A gigantosaurus.

Charlotte Irvine (7)
Hadfield Infant School, Hadfield

What Am I?

I have a short head and a short tail.
I live in North America.
I eat fish, crabs and animals.
I have sharp teeth like knives.
I have a crescent coming from my head.
I have big wings like a plane.
I don't have arms.
I move by flying very fast.
What am I?

Answer: A pterodactyl.

Ella-Rose Carter (6)
Hadfield Infant School, Hadfield

What Am I?

My name means 'arm lizard'.
My period is the Jurassic.
I weigh thirty-five tonnes.
I am a plant-eater, so I am a herbivore.
I live in Asia.
I have a long neck.
I have a long tail.
I lived two hundred million years ago.
What am I?

Answer: A brachiosaurus.

Fred Lally (7)
Hadfield Infant School, Hadfield

Years Gone By

I have razor-sharp teeth that can kill my enemy.
I have small arms as small as a pencil.
I'm twenty metres high.
I live in Canada.
I eat blood-dripping meat.
I was extinct sixty-five million years ago.
I have yellow pupils.
What am I?

Answer: A T-rex.

Oscar Marsh (6)
Hadfield Infant School, Hadfield

In A Time Gone By

You will not find me in a herd.
I have sharp teeth to rip off other dinosaurs'
flesh.
I have spikes on my back.
My body is shorter than a diplodocus.
Some of my skin is as green as a frog.
My fossils are found in England.
What am I?

Answer: A megalosaurus.

James Hurdley (6)
Hadfield Infant School, Hadfield

What Am I?

I live in North America.
I'm about as a big as a house.
My head is 1.2 metres.
I quickly hide and jump out at my prey.
I am a carnivore.
I have sharp claws.
I hatch from an egg.
I'm the king of the dinosaurs.
What am I?

Answer: A T-rex.

Thomas Lythgoe (7)
Hadfield Infant School, Hadfield

Guess My Dinosaur

I live in Canada.
I have two long legs.
I don't like to swim.
I weigh five tonnes.
I lived during the Cretaceous period.
I kind of look like a T-rex but smaller.
I have a beak-like mouth.
I have a crescent.
What am I?

Answer: A crocosaurus.

Olivia Gayle (7)
Hadfield Infant School, Hadfield

Dinosaurs Who?

I have a long tail.
I have two short arms.
I look like an iguanodon.
I live in North America.
I loudly stamp through the forest.
I quickly catch my prey.
I am a meat-eating dinosaur.
I am the king of the dinosaurs.
What am I?

Answer: A T-rex.

Sophie Lomas (7)
Hadfield Infant School, Hadfield

What Am I?

I live in Africa but I am not a cheetah.
I am fast like a tiger.
I do not fly.
I don't swim.
I have long arms like an allosaurus.
I have a bumpy back.
I am lighter than a house.
I have stompy feet.
What am I?

Answer: A spinosaurus.

Kai Andrew Barker (7)
Hadfield Infant School, Hadfield

Many Years Ago

I have been extinct many years.
I have sharp, pointy teeth like a Stanley knife.
I eat other animals because I am a carnivore.
I am as big as an elephant..
I am as long as a tennis court.
I am as long as three houses.
What am I?

Answer: A T-rex.

Gabriel Marley (6)
Hadfield Infant School, Hadfield

Dinosaurs

I have a heavy tail.
I am bigger than your hand.
I am a herbivore.
I was hatched from an egg.
I am three tonnes.
I am a metre long.
I am similar to an atlantosaurus.
I have bone plates on my back.
What am I?

Answer: A stegosaurus.

Jasmine Rebecca Hughes (6)
Hadfield Infant School, Hadfield

Years Gone By

My brain is a small as a fist.
I have a long and strong, whipping tail.
I have small feet like a human's face.
My eyes are as small as two apples.
I am twenty-two metres long.
I am found in the USA.
What am I?

Answer: A diplodocus.

Liam Hamilton (7)
Hadfield Infant School, Hadfield

What Am I?

I am a herbivore.
I live in North America during the Jurassic period,
One hundred and fifty-five million years ago.
I hatch from an egg.
I do not have spikes on my neck.
I am as long as three buses.
What am I?

Answer: A diplodocus.

Kenya Mae Lee (7)
Hadfield Infant School, Hadfield

What Am I?

I have four legs.
I have three horns.
I run at my enemy.
I live in North America.
I am a herbivore.
I have a small tail.
I am called a three-horned
Because I have three horns on my head.
What am I?

Answer: A triceratops.

Lucas Ravenscroft (7)
Hadfield Infant School, Hadfield

What Am I?

I am a meat-eater
And I am really big.
I am the king of the dinosaurs.
I have short arms like pencils.
I have sharp teeth like a dagger,
Claws like a knife.
I lay eggs.
I drink water.
What am I?

Answer: A T-rex.

Leighton Michael James Boyce (7)
Hadfield Infant School, Hadfield

Long, Long Ago

I have a lump on my head and I'm a herbivore because I eat leaves.
I live in hot places and I'm brown.
I have a small tail.
I have sharp teeth.
I move quickly.
I am strong.
What am I?

Answer: A pachycephalosaurus.

Joshua Stanley (7)
Hadfield Infant School, Hadfield

What Am I?

I live in the jungle.
I eat juicy, green plants because I'm a herbivore.
You might see me pulling down trees.
My tail is very long.
Other dinosaurs might eat me.
What am I?

Answer: A diplodocus.

Sophie Louise Willett (7)
Hadfield Infant School, Hadfield

Jurassic Park

I jump very high.
I am a carnivore.
I am in the T-rex family.
On some of my back, I have hair.
I come in peace.
My teeth are as sharp as a spike.
What am I?

Answer: An utahraptor.

Benjamin Taylor (7)
Hadfield Infant School, Hadfield

Stompy Dinosaurs

I am a herbivore.
I have spikes on my back like a stegosaurus.
I swallow stones.
I have pegged teeth.
I am as long as three giraffes' necks.
What am I?

Answer: A diplodocus.

Ryan Myers-King (6)
Hadfield Infant School, Hadfield

What Am I?

I can keep cool by using my head.
I am as big as a bus.
I eat palm leaves.
I live in a herd.
I have many teeth.
I came out of an egg.
What am I?

Answer: A triceratops.

Summer Jacqueline Maureen Heald (6)
Hadfield Infant School, Hadfield

Dinosaurs

I have very big legs.
I eat leaves off the trees.
I swallow stones to grind up my food.
I am very heavy.
I have little, sharp teeth.
What am I?

Answer: A diplodocus.

Lewis Lomas (6)
Hadfield Infant School, Hadfield

Long, Long Ago

I can keep cool by using my head.
I am as big as a bus or train.
I eat plants.
I live in a herd.
First, I was an egg.
What am I?

Answer: A triceratops.

Archie Quinlan (6)
Hadfield Infant School, Hadfield

What Am I?

I don't swim.
I lay eggs.
I live in North America.
I eat meat.
A spinosaurus eats me.
What am I?

Answer: A T-rex.

Reuben Atkinson (7)
Hadfield Infant School, Hadfield

Long, Long Ago...

I eat juicy meat quickly.
My teeth are small as knives.
You won't see me in herds.
What am I?

Answer: A T-rex.

Freddie Hughes-Couper (6)
Hadfield Infant School, Hadfield

What Am I?

I can keep cool by using my head.
I am as big as a bus.
I eat plants.
What am I?

Answer: A triceratops.

Haniya Hussain (6)
Hadfield Infant School, Hadfield

One Of Your Five A Day

I am sweet, soft and juicy.
I am red all over.
I have green hair and freckles everywhere.
I am your favourite milkshake flavour.
I am very nice with pancakes.
I am shaped like a heart full of love.
What am I?

Answer: A strawberry.

Nusaybah Naseer (6)
Normanton House School, Derby

The Silly Man

I have a little brown teddy.
We do everything together.
I have a green Mini car.
I do a lot of silly things.
I don't have friends
But I live with an old woman who has a tough cat.
Who am I?

Answer: Mr Bean.

Abdullah Mahfuz (6)
Normanton House School, Derby

Royal People

I wear jewellery.
I am always surrounded by royalty.
I wave and bow
But others don't know how.
I have a maid, steward and butler.
I can go to the village.
Who am I?

Answer: A princess.

Azka Bhatti (7)
Normanton House School, Derby

Go Fruity

I am red and I have green leaves.
I am juicy and fruity.
I am used in jams and yoghurts.
You can have one or more of me.
I grow in spring and summer.
What am I?

Answer: A strawberry.

Zahra Yasir (6)
Normanton House School, Derby

Delicious

I am yummy and sweet.
I am often a treat.
I can sometimes melt in your mouth.
I sometimes get stuck in your teeth.
Caramel is sometimes inside me.
What am I?

Answer: Chocolate.

Sumayyah Hussain (6)
Normanton House School, Derby

Humans Are Yummy

I like to climb enormous trees.
I am big and heavy like a lion.
I am fierce and strong.
I am black like a dog.
Don't come near me or else you will be my lunch.
I am really loud like a tiger.
I beat my chest like a drum.
What am I?

Answer: A gorilla.

Addison Homyard (7)
Renishaw Primary School, Sheffield

The Animal Of Spring

I can jump as high as a plane.
I've got sharp claws.
Don't come near me as I may butt you.
I like fresh grass.
I will jump on you if you come near me.
I like to jump.
I am very brown.
What am I?

Answer: A gazelle.

Scarlett Fay Green (6)
Renishaw Primary School, Sheffield

The Chatterbox

I can fly as high as an aeroplane.
What a colourful animal I am.
I will repeat you if you say a word.
Don't come near me or I will peck you with
my sharp beak.
Sometimes I like to live in trees.
What am I?

Answer: A parrot.

Ella Bradshaw (7)
Renishaw Primary School, Sheffield

The Fury Monster

I have a big, heavy hood around my head.
I have huge ears, so if you are near me, I
can hear you.
People are scared of me.
I like to eat fresh meat.
I have a short tail.
How fast I am at eating.
What am I?

Answer: A lion.

Kelsi-Rae Deakin (6)
Renishaw Primary School, Sheffield

The Crossroad Animal

Don't come near me or I will kick you.
What a lot of thin stripes I have.
I like living near cold water.
I live in a herd.
I love to eat green, juicy grass.
We all have different stripes.
What am I?

Answer: A zebra.

Edie Bonewell (7)
Renishaw Primary School, Sheffield

The Leaf Eater

My neck is as long as a skyscraper.
Never feed me meat.
How spotty I am!
I'm not a predator.
I'm a mammal.
I live in a herd.
I eat the juiciest leaves off the trees.
What am I?

Answer: A giraffe.

Pixie Pears (7)
Renishaw Primary School, Sheffield

The Fast Runner

I am as fat as a football.
I've got small horns.
How small am I!
I only eat grass as green as leaves.
Don't come near me or I will trample you.
I have very heavy feet.
What am I?

Answer: A buffalo.

Hollie Mae Williams (7)
Renishaw Primary School, Sheffield

The Fang Stabber

I am still as a crocodile.
Don't come near me because you will get stabbed.
How fierce I am.
I am a carnivore.
I am as scary as a killer clown.
I am as powerful as a whale.
What am I?

Answer: A snake.

Kai Paul Taylor (7)
Renishaw Primary School, Sheffield

High Swinger

How colourful am I?
I have a very sharp beak.
I have very sharp claws.
Don't come near me or I will grab you.
I am very fluffy.
I fly in the sky like a colourful kite.
What am I?

Answer: A parrot.

Elissa Summer Bentley (6)
Renishaw Primary School, Sheffield

The Cat Snatcher

Don't come near me or I will rip
your skin off.
I have sharp nails.
How fast I am.
I am a good hunter.
I run fast to get my prey.
How fierce I am.
What am I?

Answer: A cheetah.

Jessica Elizabeth Cusack (7)
Renishaw Primary School, Sheffield

What Am I?

I am a hairy animal.
What a horrible creature I am.
Don't come near me or you will be
breakfast.
I have teeth as sharp as knives.
I have a diet of meat.
What am I?

Answer: A lion.

Elliot Forrest (6)
Renishaw Primary School, Sheffield

The Dot Animal

I run like lightning.
I climb like lightning.
Sometimes I climb trees and look
out for prey.
My dots are like dot-to-dot.
How fast I am.
What am I?

Answer: A leopard.

Isabella Hurst (6)
Renishaw Primary School, Sheffield

Black And White

Don't come near me or I will kick you.
I am hunted by cheetahs.
I eat plants and leaves.
I am black and white.
How sad it is to be hunted.
What am I?

Answer: A zebra.

Willow-Rose Bullock (7)

Renishaw Primary School, Sheffield

Fly In The Sky

I can fly like birds.
I like to copy other people.
I live in trees.
Don't come near me or I will peck you.
I am very colourful.
What am I?

Answer: A parrot.

Miley Marie Grainger (6)
Renishaw Primary School, Sheffield

The Loud Roar

I roar really loudly.
Don't come near me or I will eat you.
My mane is like a hood.
I am a meat-eater.
My teeth are very sharp.
What am I?

Answer: A lion.

Daniel Robson (6)

Renishaw Primary School, Sheffield

The Beating Drum

I am really strong.
I love soft bananas.
Don't have a battle with me.
What huge muscles I have.
I beat my chest like a drum.
What am I?

Answer: A gorilla.

Felicity Lewis-Ord (7)
Renishaw Primary School, Sheffield

The High Jumper

I can jump as high as a kite.
Don't come near me or I might
stand on you.
Lions like to eat me.
I like juicy, green grass.
What am I?

Answer: A gazelle.

Rio Poulton (7)
Renishaw Primary School, Sheffield

What Am I?

Don't come near me or I will kick you.
I am black and white.
I love to kick.
I look like a horse.
I love my friends.
What am I?

Answer: A zebra.

Harvey Watson (6)
Renishaw Primary School, Sheffield

The Sharp Horner

I have a sharp horn.
Don't come near me.
I am as big as a statue.
I can bash you with my horn.
I am a herbivore.
What am I?

Answer: A rhino.

Callum Halliday (6)
Renishaw Primary School, Sheffield

What Am I?

I sneak up on my prey.
I am green like a leaf.
I eat fish and meat.
Don't come near me.
What am I?

Answer: A crocodile.

Damien Paul Wilkinson-Yates (7)
Renishaw Primary School, Sheffield

The Hairy One

I am very hairy.
I beat my chest.
I am king of the jungle.
I am black.
What am I?

Answer: A gorilla.

Tiffany Lindley (7)
Renishaw Primary School, Sheffield

The Caped Woman

I have a long red and stretchy cape.
I wear long red shiny big boots.
I have two shiny, sparkly bracelets which
are stronger than a bull.
My real name is Princess Diana.
I have a sparkly lasso which makes people
tell the truth.
I have a crinkly blue skirt.
I have a sparkling silver tiara.
Who am I?

Answer: Wonder Woman.

Italia Shuttleworth Fulton (7)
Stenson Fields Primary Community School, Stenson
Fields

The Super Saver!

I can fly as high as a zooming rocket.
I am as strong as an elephant.
I am as tall as a shiny, giant skyscraper.
I am as clever as a dolphin.
I can run as fast as a terrifying cheetah chasing its prey.
I am as sneaky as a sly fox.
I am as brave as a lion.
Who am I?

Answer: A superhero.

Naiya Raichura (7)
Stenson Fields Primary Community School, Stenson Fields

The Big Bang!

I can fly as fast as an eagle.
I am as strong as a dinosaur.
I can run as fast as a cheetah chasing
its food.
I am as brave as a nurse.
I am as tall as a fiery rocket.
I am as sneaky as an orange fox.
Who am I?

Answer: A superhero.

Ana Karamihaleva (6)
Stenson Fields Primary Community School, Stenson
Fields

The Pow!

I can fly as fast as a zooming jet.
I am as strong and fierce as a tiger.
I can run as fast as a spotty cheetah.
I am as brave as a hunting tiger.
I am as tall as an oak tree.
I am as sneaky as a red ant.
Who am I?

Answer: A superhero.

David Jagosz (6)

Stenson Fields Primary Community School, Stenson Fields

Out Of Space Hero

I say the thunder and lightning is at my command.
I wear a black suit.
I can fly with my hammer in my hand.
I have purple shorts.
Loki and my bad sister can hold my hammer.
I have a movie called The Dark World.
Who am I?

Answer: Thor.

Bobby Griffiths (6)
Stenson Fields Primary Community School, Stenson Fields

Brilliant Blue

I shoot lasers out of my eyes.
I can fly high in the sky like a bird.
I have supersonic hearing.
I have amazing strength.
I wear an ocean-blue suit
And a cape as red as blood.
My cousin is Superwoman.
Who am I?

Answer: Superman.

Saraya Thind (7)
Stenson Fields Primary Community School, Stenson Fields

The Suspicious Sneaky Bat

I have magnificent sidekicks, the ultimate robot.
I drive a black, shiny car.
I wear a black, leathery cloak.
I even had a fight with Superman.
I have a yellow bat on my belt.
My real name is Bruce Wayne.
Who am I?

Answer: Batman.

Myraa Khan (6)
Stenson Fields Primary Community School, Stenson Fields

What Am I?

I live in the jungle with my fantastic friends.
I have a long neck and long legs.
I have spots on my body.
I sound like *munch munch*.
I feel soft and fluffy.
I like to eat delicious leaves.
What am I?

Answer: A giraffe.

Amelia Ridley (6)

Stenson Fields Primary Community School, Stenson Fields

Caped Crusader

I have a blue skirt like the sea.
I wear a blue and red dress like the American flag.
I have a golden, shiny lasso for people to tell the truth.
I have brown hair mixed with black and it looks golden.
Who am I?

Answer: Wonder Woman.

Tilly Rose Dean (6)
Stenson Fields Primary Community School, Stenson Fields

What Am I?

I live in the damp jungle.
I look bright, yellow and I have brown spots.
I have a cute, furry tail.
I feel very, very hard and a little bit soft.
I like to eat juicy, soft leaves from the trees.
What am I?

Answer: A giraffe.

Ava Gould (6)
Stenson Fields Primary Community School, Stenson Fields

The Caped Man

I have a black and shiny grappling hook.
I have a red and yellow belt.
I live in a cold lair in a waterfall.
I have a black and shiny car which is as fast
a rocket.
I have a black and grey suit.
Who am I?

Answer: Batman.

Dylan Perkin (6)
Stenson Fields Primary Community School, Stenson
Fields

Who Am I?

My cousin is Catgirl.
I don't like meat.
I am a girl.
My boyfriend is Superman.
My enemy is Nightmare Man.
I give good dreams.
I love dreams.
My sister is Wonder Woman.
Who am I?

Answer: A superhero.

Sophia Meek (6)

Stenson Fields Primary Community School, Stenson Fields

The Super Bang

I can fly as fast as an aeroplane.
I am as strong and fierce as a tiger.
I can run as fast as a cheetah.
I am as brave as a knight.
I am as tall as Big Ben.
I am as sneaky as a fox.
Who am I?

Answer: A superhero.

Avinash Singh Takhar (7)
Stenson Fields Primary Community School, Stenson Fields

What Am I?

I live in a house with people.
I have brown fur.
I make a *woof woof* noise.
I have flappy ears.
I have black spots.
I am cute and I have blue eyes.
I have lots of friends.
What am I?

Answer: A dog.

Hollie Jennifer Pearce (5)
Stenson Fields Primary Community School, Stenson Fields

What Am I?

I live with my fantastic family.
I have a long, fluffy tail
And I wag it when I'm happy.
I love to eat amazing meat.
I am as fluffy as cotton wool.
I am as cute as a kitten
What am I?

Answer: A puppy.

Freya Mae Chorley (6)
Stenson Fields Primary Community School, Stenson
Fields

Zap! Wap! Boom!

I can fly as fast as an eagle.
I am as strong as a fierce dinosaur.
I can run as fast as a speedy cheetah.
I am as brave as a dedicated doctor.
I am as sneaky as a cute hedgehog.
Who am I?

Answer: A superhero.

Kyla Turner (7)

Stenson Fields Primary Community School, Stenson
Fields

The Super Fast Zap!

I can shoot lasers.
I can go invisible.
I can swing to the rocket.
I can breathe underwater.
I can shoot fire.
I don't have to wear anything and I don't get cold.
Who am I?

Answer: A superhero.

Shreya Dhugga (6)

Stenson Fields Primary Community School, Stenson Fields

The Pows!

I am as strong as a grey, huge elephant.
I am as quiet and squeaky as a mouse.
I am as tall as a giant skyscraper.
I am as spiky as a thorn.
I am as brave as a kind doctor.
Who am I?

Answer: A superhero.

Ethan Child (7)
Stenson Fields Primary Community School, Stenson Fields

The Amazing Pow!

I can fly as fast as a jet.
I can run as fast as a fox.
I am as strong as a tiger.
I am as brave as a crocodile.
I am as tall as a tree.
I am as sneaky as a mouse.
Who am I?

Answer: A superhero.

Ethan Dhariwal (6)
Stenson Fields Primary Community School, Stenson Fields

What Am I?

I live in the blue, wonderful sea.
I look like a silver whale.
I feel like a snake's scales.
I like to eat delicious fish.
I like to eat fish because they are tasty.
What am I?

Answer: A shark.

Ajay Janagal (6)

Stenson Fields Primary Community School, Stenson Fields

Strong Man

I have green skin as dark as an oak leaf.
I am as strong as a dump truck.
My power is saving the world.
I am a big boy.
I am very, very fat.
I wear purple leggings.
Who am I?

Answer: The Hulk

Parneet Shanan (7)

Stenson Fields Primary Community School, Stenson Fields

What Am I?

I live in the pale green rainforest.
My body has fur all over it.
I have a big, furry mane.
I roam the African wild.
I am as fluffy as a pillow.
I rule the jungle.
What am I?

Answer: A lion.

Evan Hall (6)
Stenson Fields Primary Community School, Stenson Fields

What Am I?

I live in a wonderful stable.
I have a long, fluffy tail.
I have long, soft ears.
I like to eat wonderful straw.
I make a wonderful sound which is *eeyore*.
What am I?

Answer: A donkey.

Ella Holland (5)
Stenson Fields Primary Community School, Stenson Fields

What Am I?

I live in a little basket.
I am as soft as a blanket.
I have sparkling, blue eyes.
I have a whole load of fur.
I eat very hard meat.
I have black and brown fur.
What am I?

Answer: A dog.

Skye Bareham (5)
Stenson Fields Primary Community School, Stenson Fields

The Amazing Pow!

I can fly as high as a bird.
I am as strong as an elephant.
I can run fast like a cheetah.
I am brave.
I am as tall as a tower.
I am as sneaky as a mouse.
Who am I?

Answer: A superhero.

Amelia Fulcher (6)
Stenson Fields Primary Community School, Stenson Fields

Red Speeder

I am faster than Lamborghini.
I am fifty times faster than a cheetah.
I can run to Africa and back in ten seconds.
I can see what is inside a bin by closing my eyes.
Who am I?

Answer: *The Flash.*

Rajan Singh Khatkar (6)
Stenson Fields Primary Community School, Stenson Fields

What Am I?

I live in the water.
I have skin and a shell as well.
I eat seaweed.
My shell is rock-hard.
When I am scared, I hide in my shell.
I swim across the water.
What am I?

Answer: A turtle.

Nikolai Sheppard (6)
Stenson Fields Primary Community School, Stenson
Fields

What Am I?

I live in a beautiful house with my beautiful family.
I look like a furball and I look very cute.
I purr when I am happy!
I feel like a bunny.
I like to eat tuna.
What am I?

Answer: A cat.

Freya Turner (5)
Stenson Fields Primary Community School, Stenson Fields

What Am I?

I live with my fantastic family.
I am as furry as cotton wool
And I am as cute as a puppy.
I hiss when I am angry.
I feel like wool.
I like to eat mice.
What am I?

Answer: A kitten.

Paige Buxton (6)
Stenson Fields Primary Community School, Stenson
Fields

The Big Bang!

I can fly like a bird.
I have a red cape.
I have a blue body.
I can shoot bullets.
I can fly as fast as a bird.
I can throw spikes.
I can jump high.
Who am I?

Answer: Superman.

Kenzie Maneffa (7)

Stenson Fields Primary Community School, Stenson Fields

Ace Based

I am as fast as a Bugatti Veyron.
I have lightning shooting out from my back.
I have a yellow sign.
I have a red suit.
I glow in the dark with my shiny tail.
Who am I?

Answer: The Flash.

Mitchel Samuel Victor Brownson (7)
Stenson Fields Primary Community School, Stenson Fields

Who Am I?

I swing from wall to wall.
I shoot webs out of my fist.
I have a girlfriend in real life called MJ.
I wear a red and blue suit with a black
spider in the middle.
Who am I?

Answer: Spider-Man.

Esmé Evelyn Fernley (7)
Stenson Fields Primary Community School, Stenson
Fields

The Flash Runner

I am good at running and saving people.
I can run as fast as a cheetah.
I am as brave as a policeman.
I am as quiet as a mouse.
I am as tall as a bush.
Who am I?

Answer: A superhero.

Liam Whyatt (6)
Stenson Fields Primary Community School, Stenson Fields

Amazing Arachnid

I wear blue like the sea and red like apples.
My real name is Peter Parker
Like Peter Rabbit in CBeebies.
My superpower is to shoot super-sticky,
white webs.
Who am I?

Answer: Spider-Man

Amelia (6)

Stenson Fields Primary Community School, Stenson Fields

What Am I?

I live on a farm.
I am as pink as candyfloss.
I have a curly tail.
I go *oink* when I talk to my friends.
I am very smelly.
I like to eat hay.
What am I?

Answer: A pig.

Zach Coleman-Wright (6)
Stenson Fields Primary Community School, Stenson Fields

What Am I?

I live in a beautiful, clean house.
I am as cute as a baby.
I look very fluffy.
I feel like candyfloss.
I make a *woof* sound.
I eat bones.
What am I?

Answer: A puppy.

Arniya Chopra (6)
Stenson Fields Primary Community School, Stenson Fields

Who Am I?

I have a Batsuit.
I have a strong car and strong shoes.
I have black, strong wings.
I am strong, fit and faster than a lorry.
I am faster than a Mustang.
Who am I?

Answer: Batman.

Arun Singh Mehat (6)
Stenson Fields Primary Community School, Stenson Fields

What Am I?

I am fluffy like cotton wool.
I am white like snow.
I like to go out at night.
I live in a cage.
I am little like an egg.
I like to eat brown food.
What am I?

Answer: A cat.

Olivia Rose Borrington (6)

Stenson Fields Primary Community School, Stenson
Fields

What Am I?

I live in a very dark cage.
I live in a wet cage.
I am so cheeky.
I do not like noise.
If you disturb me, I will not play.
I run on a wheel.
What am I?

Answer: A hamster.

Khloe Ann Walker (5)
Stenson Fields Primary Community School, Stenson Fields

The Big Zap

I am as fast as a snow leopard.
I have super-hearing like a bat.
I am as quiet as a hedgehog.
I am as tall as a deer.
My ancestors are cavemen.
Who am I?

Answer: A superhero.

Corben Jozef Wensierski (7)

Stenson Fields Primary Community School, Stenson
Fields

What Am I?

I live with the other animals.
I roar like a tiger.
I am very strong.
I make a roaring sound.
I am very furry and fluffy.
I like to eat meat.
What am I?

Answer: A lion.

Musaab Abdulghani Elazreg (6)
Stenson Fields Primary Community School, Stenson
Fields

What Am I?

I live in a hard shell.
I look like a sea creature.
I look like a tortoise.
I don't make any noise at all.
I am very slow.
I am green.
What am I?

Answer: A turtle.

Amber Brewin (6)

Stenson Fields Primary Community School, Stenson
Fields

What Am I?

I am a scary creature.
I can squash fingers.
I am big and strong.
I am heavy like an elephant.
I have a long neck.
I have sharp teeth.
What am I?

Answer: A dinosaur.

Olivier Siemieński (5)

Stenson Fields Primary Community School, Stenson
Fields

Caped Crusader

I have a big, black car.
My car has enormous gadgets.
I have Robin for a sidekick.
I shoot hot lasers from my eyes.
My real name is Bruce Wayne.
Who am I?

Answer: Batman.

Ethan Michael Haywood (6)

Stenson Fields Primary Community School, Stenson Fields

What Am I?

I live in a cage.
I have fur.
I will bite.
I am fluffy.
I am cute.
I need water.
I like food.
I need a walk.
I need a rest.
What am I?

Answer: A dog.

Ethan Brealey (5)
Stenson Fields Primary Community School, Stenson Fields

What Am I?

I live in the deep sea.
I am enormous.
I have sharp teeth.
I crunch my teeth when I eat people.
I feel scaly.
My favourite food is fish.
What am I?

Answer: A shark.

Tyler Baldwin (5)

Stenson Fields Primary Community School, Stenson Fields

What Am I?

I live in the water.
I have sharp teeth.
My scales are like slime.
I am green like leaves.
I have rows of teeth.
My mouth is long.
What am I?

Answer: A crocodile.

Harvey Bloor (6)
Stenson Fields Primary Community School, Stenson
Fields

The Super Person

I can fly as fast as an aeroplane.
I run as fast as a cheetah.
I'm as strong as the army.
I'm as fierce as a leopard that is angry.
Who am I?

Answer: A superhero.

Lilly May Hamilton (7)

Stenson Fields Primary Community School, Stenson Fields

What Am I?

I live in the juicy grass.
I am brown and have a tail.
I am very soft.
I like to eat grass.
I have a brown body.
You can ride me.
What am I?

Answer: A horse.

Layla Callanan (6)
Stenson Fields Primary Community School, Stenson Fields

What Am I?

I live in a little cage.
I am fluffy and cute.
Be careful, I might bite!
I am a pet.
I am soft like a rabbit.
I have blue eyes.
What am I?

Answer: A dog.

Maison Levi Squires (6)

Stenson Fields Primary Community School, Stenson Fields

What Am I?

I live in a black hole.
I am black and furry.
I eat rabbit food.
I sound like a mouse.
I can squeak.
I play as well.
What am I?

Answer: A rabbit.

Harleen Kaur-Samra (5)
Stenson Fields Primary Community School, Stenson
Fields

The Girl Of Steel

I have big, black claws.
I fight Batman.
I have got red clothes.
I have a cape.
I have a red hat.
I can shoot lasers.
Who am I?

Answer: Batgirl.

Alfie James Page (6)

Stenson Fields Primary Community School, Stenson Fields

What Am I?

I live with my fantastic family.
I look very cuddly.
My sound is miaow
And I live in a house.
I eat mice and scare people.
What am I?

Answer: A cat.

Shanice Mfarinya (5)
Stenson Fields Primary Community School, Stenson
Fields

What Am I?

I live on the ground.
I feel bumpy.
I could bite you!
I have eight legs.
I am a little creature.
I am black.
What am I?

Answer: A spider.

Reuben Kyle Pall (6)
Stenson Fields Primary Community School, Stenson
Fields

The Man Of Steel

I am as strong as steel.
I have a blue, strong and bulletproof suit.
My arch-enemies are Poison Ivy, Harley and
The Joker.
Who am I?

Answer: Superman.

Blake Horton (7)
Stenson Fields Primary Community School, Stenson
Fields

Who Am I?

I can fly like a butterfly.
I can sneak like a panther.
I can camouflage like a cheetah.
I am brave like a lion.
Who am I?

Answer: A superhero.

Ruby Horton (7)
Stenson Fields Primary Community School, Stenson Fields

What Am I?

I live in an wonderful house.
I am furry.
I sound like a bear.
I feel like a bear.
I like to eat dog food.
What am I?

Answer: A dog.

Brody Rocco Lawlor (6)
Stenson Fields Primary Community School, Stenson Fields

What Am I?

I live in a hole.
I have some fur.
I have sharp teeth.
I have long ears.
My tail is small like a dot.
What am I?

Answer: A rabbit.

Shanae Mfarinya (5)
Stenson Fields Primary Community School, Stenson Fields

What Am I?

I live in a cave.
I am king of the jungle.
I have a fierce roar.
I am fierce and wild.
I am soft.
What am I?

Answer: A tiger.

Darai Stewart-Chance (5)
Stenson Fields Primary Community School, Stenson
Fields

The Amazing Bang

I have an orange cape
And I can fly.
I'm as strong as a gorilla.
I can see everyone in danger.
Who am I?

Answer: A superhero.

Andreas Ferreira (6)

Stenson Fields Primary Community School, Stenson
Fields

Caped Crusader

I have a black cape and suit.
I am super strong.
I have a bulletproof suit.
I have a massive car.
Who am I?

Answer: Batman.

Sam Murby (6)
Stenson Fields Primary Community School, Stenson
Fields

What Am I?

I live on the farm.
I have four legs and I'm pink.
I am not very fast.
I like to eat grass.
What am I?

Answer: A pig.

Raheem Mahmood (6)

Stenson Fields Primary Community School, Stenson Fields

What Am I?

I live in a tank.
I am lots of colours.
I am scaly.
I don't make any sound.
What am I?

Answer: A fish.

Evie Read (5)
Stenson Fields Primary Community School, Stenson Fields

The Cheeky Climber

I live in the jungle.
I have brown hair.
I eat bananas.
I swing on the trees.
What am I?

Answer: A monkey.

Katelin Eason-Patilla (5)
Stenson Fields Primary Community School, Stenson Fields

The Cheeky Climber

I live in the jungle.
I have brown hair.
I eat bananas.
I swing on the trees.
What am I?

Answer: A monkey.

Aleah Shanker (5)
Stenson Fields Primary Community School, Stenson Fields

Who Am I?

I like the dark.
I have a blue cape.
I have a 'G' for a logo.
Who am I?

Answer: A superhero.

Ciaran Gilligan (7)

Stenson Fields Primary Community School, Stenson Fields

Swirly Ride

You go down me on a very rough mat.
I am about ten metres high.
I go round and round till you hit the ground.
I have a man at the top and when you get
to the top of me, it looks very high.
I've got about fifty steps and they're tricky
to get up.
It feels very scary on my swirly thing.

Answer: A helter skelter.

Finn Poyser (7)
Wirksworth Federation Of Infant Schools, North
End

The Curly Thing

I lived a long, long time ago.
I lived when the dinosaurs were around.
When I died, I got covered in mud.
I am as hard as a rock as I might be a rock.
I might be buried deep in the ground.
I can be big or small.
What am I?

Answer: A fossil.

Reece John Gregory (7)
Wirksworth Federation Of Infant Schools, North End

Hot And Fiery

My bony wings stick out.
I breathe boiling fire.
I am as red as a poppy.
I have big, sharp teeth.
I am big, mean and fierce.
I live in a dark, gloomy cave.
Come and see me if you think you are brave!
What am I?

Answer: A dragon.

Finley Flitter (6)
Wirksworth Federation Of Infant Schools, North End

The White

I'm cold.
I can only be made of snow.
I wear a hat and scarf.
If you touch me, I might fall down.
I slowly melt as the sun comes out.
I have a little, round head like a ball.
I have a fat tummy.
What am I?

Answer: A snowman.

Isaac Vega-White (6)

Wirksworth Federation Of Infant Schools, North End

The Bite

I am as stealthy as a tiger.
I have teeth like knives.
My skin is as green as grass.
I'm as quick as a bird.
I am a dinosaur, light and quick on my feet.
I have a poisonous bite.
What am I?

Answer: A velociraptor.

Billy Rooney (7)
Wirksworth Federation Of Infant Schools, North End

A Colourful Arch

I am nice and colourful.
I can be seen when it rains.
I can be seen when it's sunny.
I am like an arch in the sky.
I might have a pot of gold at the end of me.
I am seven colours.
What am I?

Answer: A rainbow.

Edward Lowery (7)

Wirksworth Federation Of Infant Schools, North
End

Oink Oink

My tail is as curly as string.
I live on a farm.
My nose looks like a button.
My fur is as pink as a human's face.
My ears flop down.
My trotters are as hard as metal.
What am I?

Answer: A pig.

Ava Sophia Bennett (6)
Wirksworth Federation Of Infant Schools, North End

Terrifying Big Cat

I hunt for food and prey.
I have stripes so no one can recognise me.
I am a carnivore, so I only eat meat.
I live in the jungle of India.
I am a type of cat but a big one.
What am I?

Answer: A tiger.

William Eaton (7)

Wirksworth Federation Of Infant Schools, North End

Cheepy Cheep

I can fly high in the sky.
I can spread my wings and glide.
I sing sweetly in the morning.
I eat wiggly worms.
I have a sharp beak.
My feathers can be colourful.
What am I?

Answer: A bird.

Anya Neve McCabe (7)
Wirksworth Federation Of Infant Schools, North End

Swoopy Animal

I swoop down to the ground and breathe out fire.
I am terrifying and scary.
You will be frightened of me.
I have wings.
I am red like planet Mars.
I am very famous in China.

Answer: A dragon.

Kieran Gregory (6)
Wirksworth Federation Of Infant Schools, North End

The Beautiful Bark

I've got a bark as loud as a lion.
I play with my toys all night and all day.
I chase cats.
I love going for walks.
I am black, white or brown.
I am cute.
What am I?

Answer: A dog.

Edith Beatrice Ford (6)
Wirksworth Federation Of Infant Schools, North End

Hoppity Hop

I am furry like silk.
I have a cotton tail.
I can bounce till I touch the clouds.
My nose is as pink as a pig.
I eat carrots for tea.
I live underground.
What am I?

Answer: A rabbit.

Maisie Ann White (7)
Wirksworth Federation Of Infant Schools, North End

The Fluffy Bark

I growl.
I love going for walks.
I like beef.
I like chasing cats.
I have a bark as loud as a lion.
I am very cute.
What am I?

Answer: A dog.

Marnie Learmouth (7)
Wirksworth Federation Of Infant Schools, North End

YoungWriters
Est.1991

YOUNG WRITERS INFORMATION

We hope you have enjoyed reading this book – and that you will continue to in the coming years.

If you're a young writer who enjoys reading and creative writing, or the parent of an enthusiastic poet or story writer, do visit our website **www.youngwriters.co.uk**. Here you will find free competitions, workshops and games, as well as recommended reads, a poetry glossary and our blog.

If you would like to order further copies of this book, or any of our other titles, then please give us a call or visit **www.youngwriters.co.uk**.

Young Writers
Remus House
Coltsfoot Drive
Peterborough
PE2 9BF
(01733) 890066
info@youngwriters.co.uk